DISCUSSING THE WORD
STUDIES DESIGNED TO PROMOTE DISCUSSION

THE
HEART
OF
PAUL

BY CHARLES WILLIS

Scripture taken from the NEW AMERICAN STANDARD BIBLE®, Copyright© 1960, 1962, 1963, 1971, 1972, 1973, 1975, 1977, 1995 by The Lockman Foundation. Used by permission. www.Lockman.org

ISBN 10: 1-58427-314-3
ISBN 13: 978-158427-314-1

truth
BOOKS

www.truthbooks.net

Guardian of Truth Foundation
CEI Bookstore
220 S. Marion, Athens, AL 35611
1-855-49-BOOKS or 1-855-492-6657
www.truthbooks.net

Table Of Contents

THE BIBLE HEART

We use a number of phrases in the English language that make reference to the heart: "You've gotta' have heart," "recite by heart," "a heartless individual," "heartsick," "heartache," "a heart to heart." All of these are accurate phrases, but they do not all discuss the same aspect of our being. The Bible also refers to different aspects of our being by using the word "heart." We are about to embark on a study of the heart of Paul and we need to understand exactly what is meant by "heart."

Chambers of the Heart

The Bible heart is comprised of four chambers which work together to make us who we are. The *emotions* are one chamber of the heart. Webster defines this as a "strong feeling." The man who "has no heart" has no emotions about the subject. So it is that we read about two men on the road to Emmaus who spoke with Christ and said of Him, "Were not our hearts burning within us while He was speaking to us on the road, while He was explaining the Scriptures to us?" (Luke 24:32). The Bible attributes many different emotions to the heart: love (1 Tim. 1:5; 1 Pet. 1:22), joy (Is. 65:14; John 16:22), pain (John 16:6), and hatred (Lev. 19:17). The Bible clearly indicates that emotions are part of our heart and play an important part in our obedience to God, but emotions are not the only means by which we gauge religious conviction. Feeling right is not the same as being right!

The *will* is a second chamber of the heart. Webster defines this as "determination." We sometimes say of a man, "his heart is not in it." 1 Corinthians 7:37 is in the context of Paul's explanations about marriage and why a father should keep his daughter from marrying. But in this context, please notice the use of the word "heart." "He who stands firm in his heart, being under no constraint, but has authority over his own will, and decided in his heart, to keep his virgin daughter, he will do well." We must see that the heart is the seat of decisions. We also know from Scripture that the heart purposes (2 Cor. 9:7), is stubborn (Ps. 81:12), and can prompt obedience (Rom. 6:17-18). A determination to do right is a function of the heart, but it is not all that is involved in religious conviction. If it were, then sincerity would be the deciding factor of salvation and that simply is not supported from Scripture.

The *intellect* is a third chamber of the heart. Webster defines this as "the ability to reason or understand." It is the reservoir of knowledge. Intelligence is based on what one has learned and knows. "Faith comes by hearing and hearing by the word of God" (Rom. 10:17). Our knowledge is learned from God's word and that is the basis of our intelligence. The intellect is also pointed out in Scripture as reasoning (Mark 2:8), pondering (Luke 2:19), belief (Rom. 10:9-10), thinking (Matt. 9:4), and understanding (Matt.13:15). The intellect must be seen as part of the Bible heart. With logic, we contemplate the things God has revealed to us regarding salvation. With purpose of mind, we rationalize and logically think through what He has commanded of us. We make a determination of our *will* based on the *intelligence* that we have gleaned as to whether or not we are right in God's sight. But, intelligence and logical thinking are not the only aspects of the Bible heart that should be considered. Otherwise, we end up like the Pharisees who observed the Law but had no love for God in what they did. The intellect allows us to worship God in truth, but "God is a spirit" and must be worshiped in "spirit and in truth" (John 4:24).

The fourth chamber of the Bible heart is the *conscience*. Webster defines this as "an awareness of right and wrong with a compulsion to do right." This is the faculty of our minds that tells us if we have done right or wrong. It is understood that what we think is right and wrong can be trained or learned; therefore, we cannot depend on our *conscience* as the only thing on which the *will* operates. *Intelligence* must be included. We are told in Scripture that our hearts can be troubled (John 14:1), condemn us (1 John 3:21), and prick us (Acts 2:36-37). So we must understand that the conscience is a vital part of the Bible heart, but it alone should not be the basis for our religious conviction. Our hearts can be clean, but they can be wrong. The Pharisees in 1 Timothy 4:2 are said to have had their "conscience seared with a hot iron" so that they were not functioning as they should (see also Tit. 1:5 and 1 Cor. 8:7). These passages demonstrate that our conscience cannot be the only guide, though some are allowing that to be the case in their lives.

All four aspects of our heart must be included in any discussion of the heart: the *emotions*, the *will*, the *intellect*, and the *conscience*. All of these will be examined in detail in this study of Paul's heart. It is hoped that through this study, we can learn better what our heart should be like so that we can serve God with all our heart, mind, and soul.

An Obedient Heart

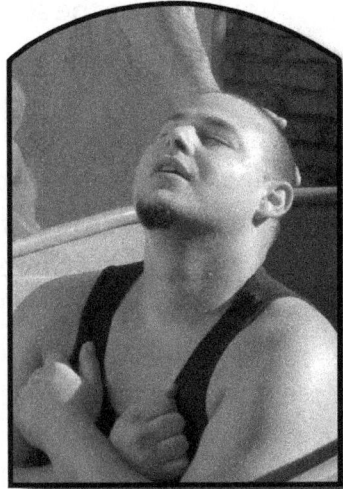

The starting place for any study about the heart must be about obedience. A heart that is unwilling to obey is not a heart with which God would be pleased. Many profitable studies could be made of men such as Noah, Moses, and Joshua, who had obedient hearts, but we are studying the heart of Paul. His attitude is best summed up in his statement, "What shall I do, Lord?" (Acts 22:10).

1. What was Paul's attitude prior to his conversion (see Acts 26:4-11 and Gal. 1:13-14)?

2. Why is this statement in Acts 22:10 so surprising, coming from Paul?

3. By this statement, what is Paul prepared to do?

4. What did Jesus want Paul to do?

5. What do Acts 26:19 and Romans 6:4 declare about his attitude?

6. Should this be the sentiment of Christians today? If it were, what more might be accomplished in the kingdom?

Paul did not enter a period of training in order to learn what was needed to preach the gospel. Some believe Galatians 1 may indicate that he spent a period of three years studying, but we must not forget that he was given the gift of the Holy Spirit which guided him into all truth and gave him a full understanding of the gospel. Yet his attitude continued to be one of obedience, even after he became an apostle. Though he was inspired of God, he still had the choice of obeying or not. We often think of Peter in this regard when Paul confronts him about his hypocritical conduct (Gal. 2), but Paul also demonstrates his struggle with sin in Romans 7:15-25 (read).

7. What statements of Paul demonstrate that he continues to have an obedient attitude?

8. What does Paul teach about obedience in Romans 6:16-17? Can we see this in his life?

Like all men, Paul had goals, aspirations, and plans. At all times, our plans should be in accordance with God's will. We know from Paul's life that his plans drastically changed. The entire course of his life changed in order to be obedient to God. As we've already examined, Jesus called him to preach to the Gentiles. We know very little about the specifics in how Paul went about fulfilling that command, but what we do know is very revealing.

9. Read the following passages and comment on how they indicate Paul's obedient attitude (Acts 16:6; 10; 2 Cor. 2:12; Rom. 1:10; 1 Thess. 3:11).

10. As Christians, we also make plans and have dreams. How does the attitude of obedience affect those personal goals?

If Paul could become obedient to God's plan of salvation, then anyone can. He serves as a permanent reminder that we can never be so far from God that He is not willing to forgive us. An attitude of obedience is necessary. He also teaches us that obedience is not accomplished once, but is an attitude that we cultivate and live with the rest of our lives. Are we living up to Paul's standard? "I wrote that I might put you to the test, whether you are obedient in all things" (2 Cor. 2:9).

11. What type of things might we have trouble obeying today?

A SUBMISSIVE HEART

Obedience (lesson 1) and submission go hand in hand. You cannot have one without the other. Every indication from Scripture is that Paul submitted his will to the Lord and adopted the Lord's will as his own. Jesus teaches that we are to deny ourselves, take up our cross, and follow Him. No one exemplifies these traits more than the apostle Paul.

1. Read 1 Corinthians 11:1 and Philippians 3:17.
    A. In what ways did Paul imitate Christ?

    B. In what ways are we to imitate Paul?

2. In context, how was Christ living in Paul (Gal. 2:20)?

3. List two areas in which we are to deny ourselves. (Pick two with which you have trouble.) Did Paul deal with these in any way (give references)?

Paul took the idea of submitting himself to God and lived in such a way that many today would have called him extreme. His life-style was such that people could see that he was a Christian. Those who knew him prior to his conversion were repulsed by his fanaticism for preaching the gospel of Jesus Christ. His teaching remains difficult today, some in thought, but most are easily understood, just hard to implement.

4. What do these passages teach about Paul's heart (Rom. 6:6; Gal. 5:24; 6:14)?

5. To crucify the world, how much of the world do we have to give up? What should be our attitude if we would be pure in heart?

Paul endured more hardship than many men. It would be difficult for us to read about his life and consider it pleasant. Paul was not concerned with what others thought about him. Though he was scorned, beaten, and chased out of town, his attitude of submitting to the Lord never changed. He was not swayed by physical forces. He seems almost inhuman in this regard, but he was a man just like us. The difference was in his attitude. Perhaps ours needs some adjustment. Read Romans 8:12-14 and notice the "we" Paul uses. Be sure to understand the full context of this setting. You may wish to read beginning in verse 5.

6. Describe the contrast between living according to the flesh versus being led by the Spirit of God.

7. How are we led by the Spirit of God today?

8. How do we put to death the deeds of the body?

Paul helps us some in understanding fully the concept of submission. He makes it very personal. It is not just a submission of one's will to the doctrine of Christ, though that is included. It is not just an initial obedience to the plan of salvation, though that is also included. Read 1 Corinthians 9:27.

9. What does it mean to buffet our body? How do we make it our slave?

10. Which parts of the Bible heart will be involved in making this happen (see *Introduction*)?

11. In your own words describe the type of submission Paul's life indicates that we should give to the Lord, especially if we are going to imitate Paul.

12. How did Jesus demonstrate submission?

13. If we fail to submit to Christ to the same extent as Paul, is that a big problem? In other words, must we submit as fully as Paul did?

14. Our submission is seen by Paul as a voluntary slavery (Rom. 6:16-23). If we are the slaves of Christ, what will be the attitude of our heart toward His will?

Paul wrote many instructions to slaves and slave owners teaching them to submit to God in the state they were in (Eph. 6:5-9; Col. 3:22-24). He also had much to say to husbands, wives, and children about submission to God and submission to the roles that God has given us (1 Cor. 7:1-5, 39; Col. 3:18-21; Eph. 5:22-31; 6:1-4). Paul writes of submission to the elders (Acts 20:28; 1 Tim. 5:17-19), submission to the governing authorities (Rom. 13:1-7), and submission to the teaching of the apostles (1 Cor. 15:1-2). His entire life was one of submission and his view toward serving God was greatly influenced by the concepts of submission. Any study of his life will easily prove that he practiced what he preached! The reason he lived in this way and taught as he did was because of the attitude of his heart. We all need the submissive heart of Paul.

AN HUMBLE HEART

Perhaps more than any other man, Paul recognized and appreciated the saved relationship he enjoyed in Christ Jesus. He never forgot where he came from (out of sin) to become the ambassador for Christ. He understood completely that it was because of God's grace that he was able to proclaim the good news to others and be right with God. "By the grace of God I am what I am" (1 Cor. 15:10). His heart was such that "grace" was a topic that created a continuous sense of humility in him.

1. What does Paul say of himself in 1 Corinthians 15:9? How does this compare with 1 Timothy 1:15?

2. Based on 2 Corinthians 12:11 and Ephesians 4:3, what was Paul's attitude about himself in God's great plan?

3. Was this just an outward show for Paul? Was this truly in his heart? What other examples could be cited as examples of Paul's humility?

4. What does the New Testament say about the boastful man?

5. Must a Christian be humble to be pleasing to God (give references)?

Humility is perhaps the hardest Christian attribute for any of us to attain. Once we think we are humble, we are not. It is so easy to allow pride to overtake us and creep into our thoughts and language. Paul was a man just like us, but his heart and attitude were humble.

6. God forgets sin. Should we? Is this what kept Paul humble?

7. Though he was an apostle, Paul never let the saints forget his humanity. What Scriptures could we point to that demonstrate Paul presented himself as a fallible man?

One of the strongest New Testament teachings about humility is presented by Paul in Philippians 2:4-5 (read). The man who considered himself the least of the Christians and the chief of sinners put Christ before us as our example.

8. How did Christ humble Himself before God?

9. Is it possible for us to have a heart of humility like Christ? Like Paul?

10. What hinders us from being humble? Why is this trait so incredibly difficult?

Paul writes a lot about the grace of God in Romans, Galatians, and elsewhere. The reason for this is because of his humility. He never forgot that he persecuted the early church. He understood all too well where his eternal destination would be without God's grace. His humility is a strength of his character and one of the things we admire in him, just as we do in Christ. Our hearts also need to be humble. We need to learn from Paul's example!

A COMMITTED HEART

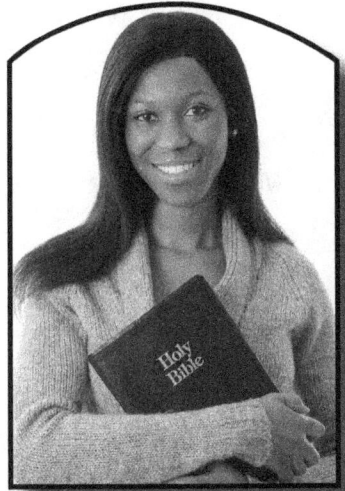

Commitment as used in this lesson is the fourth definition in Webster's dictionary, "to bind, as by a promise or pledge." The commitment Paul made to God, when he obeyed the gospel, led him to make the statement, "I am debtor" (King James) or "I am under obligation both to the Greeks and to the barbarians, both to the wise and the foolish. Thus for my part, I am eager to preach the gospel to you also who are in Rome" (Rom. 1:14-15).

1. Why did Paul feel as if he was a debtor to these people? What made him feel like he was under obligation?

2. Is there anyone to whom we should feel indebted to teach the gospel? Is there anyone to whom we are under obligation?

As we examine Paul's heart, he has told us many things about his attitude and feelings. Romans serves as an example of Paul revealing himself. In Romans 10:1 he says, "Brethren, my heart's desire and prayer to God for them is for their salvation".

3. To whom was Paul referring? What does he go on to say about them?

4. Why would Paul so strongly desire to see them saved?

5. What is our heart's desire?

   We learn from Paul that a proper attitude of heart is to be concerned for others. Salvation of others was his heart's desire. We know he left all that he had been in Jerusalem and began teaching Jesus. To the best of our knowledge, he never owned many possessions but spent his years traveling and teaching others. He had the committed heart of a servant.

6. Using John 9:4 as a starting point, compare the attitude of Paul's heart with that of Christ. Cite a few passages that support your statements.

7. What strength of commitment did the church in Laodicea possess (Rev. 3:14-22)? What type of commitment were they told to possess by Christ?

8. Upon what does Christ gauge our commitment?

9. After reading Acts 21:13, tell how Paul lived up to Jesus' statements about commitment in Luke 9:57-62 and Luke 14:25-35.

   Paul's commitment was absolute. There was no hypocrisy, no shrinking back. His was the full commitment that Jesus expects from His followers. No one can study Paul's life (or the insights into his heart) without being impressed by his full commitment. We must work toward having this attitude in ourselves.

Lesson 5

A TEACHER'S HEART

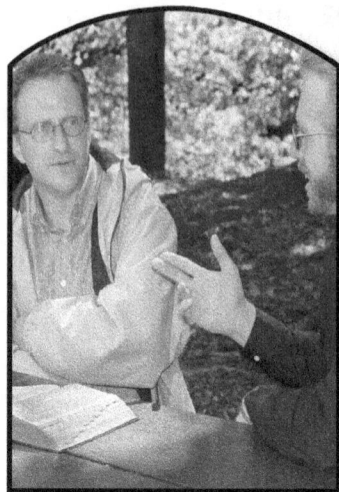

We are given a lot of information about Paul's teaching: his topics, his usual custom when arriving in a town, his use of Old Testament Scriptures as proofs, his sincerity, even his various approaches to different audiences. With all this information we never lose sight of the fact that Paul had a teacher's heart. This is best summed up in his statement, "we preach not ourselves, but Christ Jesus." Read the entire context of this passage (2 Cor. 4:4-15) and answer the following questions.

1. What does Paul say God revealed to his heart (v. 6)? What word does Paul use to describe this revelation?

2. There is a lot of language about the persecutions that Paul endured. Why does Paul say he kept on speaking of these things?

Paul was a driven man. He understood the commission given to him by the Lord and he purposed in his heart to fulfill that mission. Read 1 Corinthians 9:16-23.

3. What "compelled" Paul? Does faith necessitate that we teach others?

4. How does verse 19 indicate the attitude of his heart?

5. Please explain what Paul means in verses 20-22 by "becoming" like others. How do we use a similar method today?

Paul never tried to deceive anyone in his teaching. His motives were always pure and right (as indicated in 1 Thess. 2). We do not read where Paul was often misunderstood, though Peter tells us some of his written teaching was difficult, which the unlearned "distort" (2 Pet. 3:16). Read and be prepared to discuss Paul's statements about himself.

6. Romans 15:14-20
   A. How was Paul's attitude like a "priest" (v. 16)?

   B. What was Paul's "aspiration" (v. 20)? Why?

   C. What is meant by the phrase "fully preached the gospel of Christ" (v. 19)?

7. Acts 20:18-27
   A. Do we ever "shrink from declaring" something profitable? If so, why?

   B. What is the "whole purpose of God" that Paul taught?

8. What was the attitude of his heart as he testified these things (see also verses 24 and 31)?

Paul's attitude about teaching is perhaps best demonstrated when he confronted Peter. Read Galatians 2:11-21.

9. Paul considered himself the apostle born out of season. Peter was seen as one of the most outspoken of the apostles. How does the relating of this event demonstrate Paul's attitude to teach others?

10. What causes us to be reluctant or hesitant to approach an erring brother? What will a heart to teach compel us to do?

Jesus is the master teacher. Paul imitated Christ. We would do well to imitate his attitude toward teaching, as well as his methods!

Lesson 6

A CLEAR HEART

It is absolutely true that we must be sincere in our belief. God is a Spirit and must be worshipped in spirit and in truth. The right attitude must be maintained and the correct motivation must exist. As I stated in the introduction to this study, the Bible heart is comprised of four chambers, one of which is the *conscience*. Throughout his writings, Paul has a great deal to say about the conscience. As we are trying to examine his heart, we must take into account Paul's attitudes and teachings about his conscience. In strong statements, Paul asserts, "I have lived my life with a perfectly good conscience before God up to this day" (Acts 23:1), "I serve with a clear conscience the way my forefather did" (2 Tim. 1:3), and hold "to the mystery of faith with a clear conscience" (1 Tim. 3:9).

1. Why would this statement (Acts 23:1) appear to be strange coming from Paul?

2. Can a person's conscience be wrong? Consider Paul's life. Is the conscience trainable? If so, how is this accomplished (study Heb. 5:14)?

3. Does hypocrisy relate in any way with keeping a good conscience? If so, how?

Paul's confidence in keeping his conscience clean was so strong that in Romans 9:1 he says his conscience bears him "witness in the Holy Spirit". This degree of personal integrity (to not violate his own conscience) is something every Christian needs to adopt. Accomplishing it is not always easy.

4. Acts 24:16 is very similar to 1 Peter 3:16's "keep a good conscience". What do we learn about Paul's daily habit in regards to his conscience? How is this done?

5. Personal honesty is a concept that eludes many Americans. Many deceive themselves, including Christians. That is why it is important that we try to adopt the heart of Paul. What did Paul say needed to be done for conscience's sake (Rom. 13:5)?

Many of the passages written by Paul in regards to the conscience are dealing with the concept of eating meat that had been sacrificed to idols. Some Christians thought this was sinful and felt it would be a violation of their conscience to eat this meat. Paul says we each must obey our own conscience and that nothing God has made for food is unclean.

6. Read the following passages and be prepared to discuss Paul's revealed attitude about the conscience as well as our attitude toward others.
    A. Romans 14:1-5, 12, 14, 20-23

B. 1 Corinthians 8:7-12

C. 1 Corinthians 10:25-31

7. According to Paul, what is the danger in violating our conscience (1
Tim. 4:2; Tit. 1:15)?

8. Paul states the goal of his instruction in 1 Timothy 1:5 (speaking of
all godly instruction because of the use of "our"). How do these three
things relate and what role does the conscience play?

Purity of heart, as seen in the last question, is also called "blessed" by the
Lord in Matthew 5:8. There is no possible way to be pure in heart without
a clean conscience. Guilt of sin must be removed. Personal standards of
righteousness must be maintained. The high calling of God demands a
personal righteousness to which we must adhere. God's standards may
be our limit or our minimum, but these commands must be observed
regardless. Paul's attitude about the conscience is in perfect agreement
with 1 John 3:21, "if our heart does not condemn us, we have confidence
before God".

9. What if our heart does condemn us? How does this indicate we will
feel as we stand before the judgment seat of God?

A LOVING HEART

One of the greatest chapters in all of the Bible was written by Paul on the subject of love. 1 Corinthians chapter 13 is applicable to all relationships and is a marvelous example of inspirational writing! What must not be overlooked is that Paul held the exact attitudes of love that are expressed in this chapter. It is hoped, through a study of many of Paul's statements and teachings, that we can learn that biblical love is possible in our lives as it was in Paul's. For the purpose of study, this lesson is divided into varying aspects of love revealed in Paul's life. 1 John 3-4 teaches the principle of brotherly love as a fundamental necessity for the child of God. Through Paul's writings it is hoped we can learn more of the particulars in how this is accomplished.

See to the Interests of Others

1. Please read the following and write down the key concept of love in each verse.

    A. 1 Corinthians 10:24

    B. Philippians 2:4

    C. 1 Corinthians 9:19

D. 2 Corinthians 12:5

E. Galatians 5:13-14

2. How does this compare with our attitudes about others? Do we generally think or ourselves as slaves and servants who are gladly spent? If not, what is our attitude?

Give No Offense
3. What does Paul say?
    A. 2 Corinthians 6:3

    B. Romans 14:21

    C. 1 Corinthians 8:13

4. If love is the motivation for not causing a brother to stumble, what attitude is shown when we cause the stumbling anyway? How might we cause a brother to stumble today?

Hypocrisy and Concern
5. What two attributes of love does Paul teach must be a part of the Christian's personality?
    A. Romans 14:19

    B. Romans 12:9

6. Love for others will cause great concern, especially if there is sin in their life. Paul's heart conveyed this type of love for others. What words or phrases relate those concepts in the following verses?
   A. 2 Corinthians 2:4

   B. Philippians 1:7

   C. Though no specific phrases are used, also consider Paul's actions in Galatians 2:11-18.

   D. Why do we not express our love for each other as Paul did? What excuses or preventions do we perceive?

Examples of Paul's Love

7. Read these passages, then answer if Paul's love for them seems to be genuine, hypocritical, personal, or just as a part of the church, a result of a close or passing relationship (1 Thess. 3:12; Rom. 16:8; Phil. 4:1; 1 Cor. 16:24)?

Conclusion

8. Reading and studying all these things about Paul's heart to love is rewarding, but now we must think. How do these things hold up in Acts 15:37-41? Does Paul have a loving heart?

9. While it is not feasible to compare Paul's life to every statement found in 1 Corinthians 13, describe why you believe he is or is not a good example of the following points.

   A. Verse 4

   "Love is patient"

   "Love is not jealous"

   "Love does not brag and is not arrogant"

   B. Verse 5

   "Love is not provoked"

   "Love does not take into account wrong suffered"

   C. Verse 7

   "Love believes all things, hopes all things"

   D. Verse 8

   "Love never fails"

Paul's attitude was to love others. His love was clearly conveyed in what he said, and in his actions toward others. It permeates all of his writings, even when he is rebuking someone. Without love, many of the works of God are without profit (1 Cor. 13:1-3). Paul indicates love is vital to the attitude of the Christians. "But now abide faith, hope, love, these three; but the greatest of these is love" (1 Cor. 13:13). We all need to pursue love in our own heart as well as with others.

A CONTENTED HEART

America and materialism seem to go hand in hand. Many non-Americans believe the culture of the United States is synonymous with materialism. It is easy for Christians to be caught up in materialistic thinking, perhaps without even realizing it. Happiness, according to our culture, is directly linked to the procurement and possession of this world's things, so without them a person feels disadvantaged. This is not at all the attitude of Paul. He said, "I have learned to be content in whatever circumstances I am" (Phil. 4:11).

1. Read the complete context in Philippians 4:10-13.
    A. How is contentment learned?

    B. Paul knew how to get along "with humble means", going hungry and suffering need. How are we to "get along" in similar circumstances?

    C. Paul also knew the prosperity and abundance we are surrounded with. Is there a "proper" way to live with wealth? What is it?

    D. What is "the secret" to getting along in all situations?

2. Of what is contentment the opposite (Heb. 13:5-6)? How do the Old Testament quotes in verses 5-6 apply? What does it mean for us?

3. If "the love of money is the root of all sorts of evil" (1 Tim. 6:10-11), what does that imply about contentment?

    A. What is Paul's instruction to Timothy?

    B. Do we do this or try to get as much as we can?

4. Read 2 Corinthians 12:7-10.
    A. Provide a modern example for each of the five things in which Paul says he was content.

    B. "When I am weak, then I am strong" (v.10). Please explain. How then are we to be strong?

    C. Why are we content in these things?

5. What is the minimum Paul says we are to be content with (1 Tim. 6:6-8)?

   A. What is the context from verses 3-5?

   B. What teaching of Christ does this sound like?

   C. How much do Americans work to conform to this attitude?

6. It is not sinful for a Christian to acquire wealth. It is the love of money that is warned against. What other important considerations do these passages teach that all of us need to heed?
   A. Matthew 13:22

   B. Luke 8:14

   C. James 5:2

   D. 1 Timothy 6:17

   E. Luke 6:24

In all these passages Paul links the concept of contentment with "godliness" (1 Tim. 6:6), the "power of Christ" dwelling in us (2 Cor. 12:9), the root of goodness (1 Tim. 6:10-11), and Christ being with us (Phil. 4:13). Confidence in this life is grounded in our salvation in Jesus. Rather than trusting in the riches that fade away, we are to lay up for ourselves treasure in heaven. Our confidence, our happiness, is in knowing we are right with God. By this we learn to be content as we look for the promised reward. Contentment was an active attribute in Paul's heart and should be in ours.

A DISCIPLE'S HEART

Of all the people in the world who disbelieved, Paul was perhaps the greatest. He considered himself to be the chiefest of sinners. He was not a skeptic who had doubts, nor was he someone who just needed a little convincing. Paul did not believe and did everything in his power to convince others not to believe, even inflicting punishment on those who believed. This same man became completely convinced of the reality of Jesus being the Son of God and became obedient to the things He commanded. Paul said, "We walk by faith and not by sight" (2 Cor. 5:7). His heart became submerged in faith.

1. What does it mean to "walk by faith and not by sight" in context?

2. If Paul could have a heart of faith, what hope do we have of having a heart of faith?

Read 2 Corinthians 4:13-14

3. Our faith should result in what?

4. From the preceding verses (7-12), why do we strongly believe Paul had a heart of faith?

5. From Romans 1:16-17 what indication do we have that Paul had this attitude of heart?

6. Why does Paul say he is not ashamed of the gospel (2 Tim. 1:12)?

Throughout the Roman letter Paul teaches about the importance of faith. For example, he says "a man is justified by faith apart from works of the law" (3:8), and "having been justified by faith, we have peace with God through our Lord Jesus Christ" (5:1). He continues saying, "If you confess with your mouth Jesus as Lord, and believe in your heart that God raised Him from the dead, you shall be saved; for with the heart man believes, resulting in righteousness, and with the mouth he confesses, resulting in salvation" (10:9-10). It is obvious to the reader that Paul's faith was exactly what he described.

7. When all of his writings are considered, does Paul promote, teach, or give the impression that a man is saved by "faith only" as so many people claim? Provide proof from Scripture.

8. Read what Jesus told His disciples in John 15:18-21, then cite how Paul lived up to the reality of faithfulness. Compare also with Jesus' words to Ananias in Acts 9:15-16, as well as his "trustworthy statement" in 2 Timothy 2:11-13.

The heart of faith that Paul possessed required him to conform his life to the image of Christ (see 1 Cor. 11:1) and he encouraged others to imitate him (Phil. 3:17; Eph. 5:1; 1 Cor. 4:16).

9. Provide three examples of how we are to imitate Christ.

10. If others were to imitate our faith, what would be the state of the church?

   A. Provide both positive and negative examples of how younger Christians imitate the faith of older Christians.

   B. How can older Christians provide a good example for others to follow?

"O to be like Thee! Blessed redeemer: this is my constant longing and prayer;
Gladly I'll forfeit all of earth's treasures, Jesus, Thy perfect likeness to wear.
O to be like Thee! Blessed Redeemer, pure as Thou art;
Come in Thy sweetness, come in Thy fullness;
Stamp Thine own image deep on my heart."

Those words were penned by William Kirkpatrick in 1897 and are a good reflection of many of the themes in this lesson. The heart of confident faith desires above everything else to be like Christ. Paul underwent a tremendous change when he decided to follow Jesus. We can see how the change went deeply into his heart and was not superficial. He believed from the depths of his heart, and that foundation of faith caused him to live righteously, teach others, and obey Jesus' word. How desperately we all need the heart of faith that Paul possessed.

A PRAYING HEART

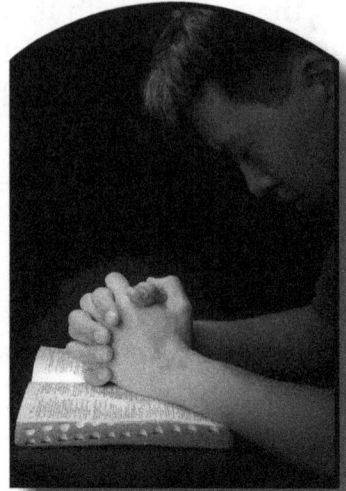

Perhaps more than any other trait, prayer is a true indicator of our heart. Though public prayer could be considered, the private prayer in our "closet" is the one we need to think about. The frequency and intensity of our prayers directly reflect our dependence on God and belief in the effectiveness of prayer. Through his writings, Paul reveals he has a praying heart.

1. Paul's introductory remarks are virtually the same in the different letters contained in Scripture. Please fill in the following chart.

Passage	Words that indicate frequency of prayer	Phrases that are different
Eph. 1:16		
Phil. 1:4		
Col. 1:3, 9		
Rom. 1:9-10		
1 Thess. 1:2		

Passage	Words that indicate frequency of prayer	Phrases that are different
2 Thess. 1:11		
2 Tim. 1:3		
Philemon 4		

Just from these simple common phrases we get an understanding that prayer was an important part of Paul's life. His frequency was more than once a day and his prayers had some repetition. But Scripture reveals so much more about Paul's heart through his example and teaching. In many of the statements above, Paul mentions "our" prayers, referring to the group of men who traveled with him teaching the gospel, but Paul also spoke of his personal prayers as in Philippians 1:9, "I pray" and Acts 16:25 when he and Silas prayed at midnight in the prison.

2. Paul believed strongly in the power of prayer. Relate and comment what the following passages reveal of his confidence in prayer.
   A. Acts 21:5

   B. Acts 20:36

3. With these concepts in mind, we now examine the teaching of Paul. What does he teach in these passages about prayer?
   A. Colossians 4:2

   B. Ephesians 6:18

   C. Philippians 4:6

   D. Romans 12:12

   E. 1 Timothy 2:8

F. 1 Thessalonians 5:17

4. Based on Paul's attitudes, comments and teaching on prayer, what do the following ideas relay about our confidence in prayer?

   A. Prayer is a public aspect of worship only, at least that is the reality in some Christian's lives.

   B. Prayer is for times of emergency and great concern.

   C. Personal prayers are offered daily at meals.

   D. "The effective prayer of a righteous man can accomplish much" (James 5:16).

   E. Seven days without prayer makes one weak.

5. What other statements in Scripture sound like 2 Timothy 4:16?

   We understand that prayer needs to be from the heart, but through the teaching and example of Paul, we learn that the disposition of the Christian heart is to frequently speak to God about all that is going on in his life. Do we have a praying heart?

A STRONG HEART

We are impressed with the faith of Paul. When situations presented themselves in his life where most men would have backed away, Paul demonstrates a strength of heart to which we relate with great difficulty. No matter what his circumstances, his zeal and confidence remained with him to continue preaching to others. When he was in prison, he wrote Timothy to encourage him and said, "For God has not given us a spirit of timidity, but of power and love and discipline. Do not be ashamed of the testimony of our Lord, or of me His prisoner but join with me in suffering for the gospel according to the power of God" (2 Tim. 1:7-8). Twice in this passage, he writes of the power of God, which is tells where he placed his confidence.

1. Paul told the Philippians, "I can do all things through Him who strengthens me" (Phil. 4:13).

    A. Please cite two or three things Paul was able to do because of his confidence in God.

    B. What kind of things are we able to do?

2. Paul has remarked several times about the strength he has in God.

   A. Read Ephesians 6:10. How can we be strong in the Lord? What is meant?

   B. Read 2 Timothy 4:16-18. In what way did God strengthen him?

   C. Read 2 Corinthians 3:1-12. What words or phrases are used to indicate this strength in God?

   D. Read 2 Corinthians 5:6-8. What caused the courage he had?

3. Paul gets more specific in the following passages. For each reference describe why we are able to be strong through Christ.

   A. 2 Timothy 2:1

   B. 2 Timothy 1:12

   C. 2 Corinthians 4:1-2

   D. 2 Corinthians 12:9-10

4. Paul taught that we could and should have this same strength of heart. Read Colossians 1:10-11 and Romans 8:31. Is this strength of heart something only the mature in Christ are able to possess? Why or why not?

5. As a man, we know Paul was discouraged by events in his life, but he never lost his "courage" or strength of faith. What causes us to not have the strength of faith, courage, and zeal that we should?

6. From 2 Corinthians 4:16-18, what do we need to do in order not to lose heart? How is this accomplished?

As believers we should have the same strength of faith as Paul because we have also become the children of God. Confidence and zeal are a result of the real hope we have in Christ Jesus. We can say with Paul, "If God be for us, who can be against us?" Nothing can separate us from the love of God (Rom. 8:35-39), and that simple fact generates great assurance and strength to our faith.

A PURPOSE-FILLED HEART

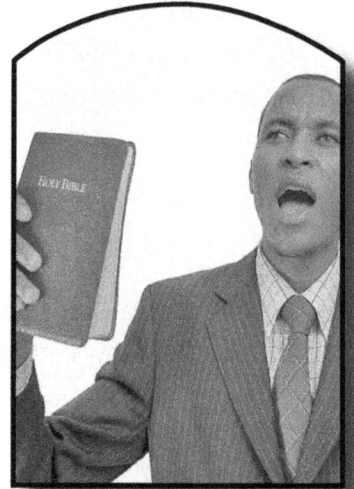

Commitment. That is what we see so evident in the heart of Paul. He was a man who had his sights set on heaven and every aspect of his being was directed toward righteousness in fulfillment of God's commands. Unless we adopt this attitude in our heart, it is unlikely that we will be received into heaven!

1. Paul completely understood the importance of setting goals. Read Philippians 3:13-15.

    A. How does humility relate to this goal?

    B. How much of "what lies ahead" should we forget? Why forget this?

    C. What is meant by "pressing" toward the goal, and how do you and I do that?

    D. Who does Paul say should have this attitude?

E. What is the prize? How does this correlate with Paul's teaching of being saved by grace? A prize seems to indicate something earned.

2. No matter what happened in his life, Paul maintained his focus on the goal. This is in part what gave him a strength of faith many do not have today. What concepts helped Paul stay focused on the goal?
   A. Romans 8:18

   B. 2 Timothy 4:18

   C. Philippians 1:21

   D. What causes us to lose our focus?

3. One of the most telling passages about Paul is 1 Corinthians 9:24-27. Read the passage and be prepared to discuss the following.
   A. "Running to win" demands "self control in all things", especially since we receive an "imperishable" crown. Discuss how goal setting, commitment, and self-control are interconnected.

   B. Is self-control instantly possible the moment we believe or does it grow? If it grows, describe how.

   C. "Running to win" speaks strongly of purpose and determination. How do these concepts stand up to the claims of the world that we are "once saved, always saved" and that a believer can "never fall away"?

D. The similarity in thought between this passage and the previous passages in this lesson cannot be ignored. Paul again emphasizes the need to keep focused on the goal, just like a runner. What do we do that would fulfill the statement "run in such a way that you may win"?

E. Where does verse 27 tell us the real struggle of faithfulness is fought?

Paul's heart is revealed in a marvelous way in Scripture. Through these passages we are shown the kind of heart we should have, and through self-examination we see how much work remains for us to do. The picture is clearly drawn for us, in that if we determine in our heart to enter into heaven, nothing can prevent us. The only one who can defeat us is ourselves. If the desire is strong enough, we can achieve anything through Jesus. Each of us must do all that is within his power to increase his desire to "win" heaven. If this trait exists, all the other traits will develop and God will be pleased. Never lose sight of the goal. That simple truth will help us immensely!

END OF STUDY REVIEW

To test your knowledge on the things studied,
attempt to answer these questions without looking back
through the workbook. If you need to look back, do so.

1. What was Paul's attitude about serving God both before and after his conversion?

2. Paul's conversion and life reflected three attributes which we studied in the first three lessons. Name them.

3. The church in Laodicea possessed a commitment that was very poor (Rev. 3:15-22, neither cold nor hot). What language does Paul use to describe his commitment (lessons 4-5)?

4. Paul would have us understand that being ashamed of the gospel is a result of which of the following:
   A. Not knowing God's word
   B. A lack of faith
   C. A lack of zeal

5. What did Paul relate to us about his conscience? How important is our conscience in regard to our salvation?

6. In lesson seven we examined many statements and teachings written by Paul in regards to love. Which of the following conveys the essence of Paul's teaching:
   A. Be concerned about others first
   B. Love those who love us
   C. Think of ourselves as the slave of others
   D. Tell others we love them
   E. Give no offense
   F. Love your enemy

7. According to Paul (lesson 8) what is the secret to contentment?

8. What does it mean to "walk by faith and not by sight" (2 Cor. 5:7, lesson 9)?

9. What can we determine about the frequency and content of Paul's prayers (lesson 10)?

10. Philippians 4:13 describes the theme of lesson eleven about *"A Strong Heart"*. What does this passage say and where does Paul indicate our strength comes from?

11. What was the purpose of Paul's life (lesson 12)?

12. Discuss how this study has been important and helpful to you.

www.ingramcontent.com/pod-product-compliance
Lightning Source LLC
Chambersburg PA
CBHW030307030426
42337CB00012B/625